Mastering the Art of Performance: A Student's Perspective

Lars Jensen

Copyright © [2023]

Title: Mastering the Art of Performance: A Student's Perspective

Author's: Lars Jensen.

This book was printed and published by [Publisher's: Lars Jensen] in [2023]

ISBN:

TABLE OF CONTENTS

Chapter 1: Introduction to Performance Art

The Definition and Evolution of Performance Art

Performance art is a dynamic and captivating form of artistic expression that challenges traditional boundaries of visual arts, theater, and dance. In this subchapter, we will explore the definition and evolution of performance art, shedding light on its historical roots and its significance in contemporary society. Designed specifically for students in the field of Performance Studies, this chapter aims to provide a comprehensive understanding of the art form and its multifaceted nature.

First and foremost, it is crucial to establish a clear definition of performance art. Unlike traditional art forms, performance art is ephemeral, existing only in the moment of its creation. It combines elements of visual art, music, dance, theater, and other artistic disciplines to convey a concept or provoke an emotional response. Performance art often blurs the line between the artist and the audience, encouraging viewer participation and interaction.

The evolution of performance art can be traced back to the early 20th century, where artists began experimenting with unconventional ways of expressing themselves. One of the pioneers of performance art was the Futurist movement, which emerged in Italy in the early 1900s. Futurists embraced technology and the industrial age, incorporating elements of movement, sound, and light into their performances.

In the mid-20th century, performance art gained momentum with the emergence of the Fluxus movement. Fluxus artists rejected the notion of art as a commodity and sought to break down the boundaries between art and everyday life. Their performances often involved absurd and humorous actions, challenging the traditional notions of what constitutes art.

Performance art reached its zenith in the 1960s and 1970s, with artists like Marina Abramovic, Yoko Ono, and Joseph Beuys pushing the boundaries of the art form. Abramovic, known for her endurance-based performances, explored the limits of the human body and the power of vulnerability. Ono's "Cut Piece" invited audience members to participate by cutting off pieces of her clothing, questioning the power dynamics between artist and spectator.

In recent years, performance art has continued to evolve and adapt to the changing social and political landscape. Artists are increasingly using the medium to address issues such as gender, race, and identity, while also incorporating digital technologies into their performances.

Studying performance art provides students with a unique perspective on the power of creativity and its ability to challenge societal norms. By examining the history and evolution of performance art, students gain a deeper understanding of the artistic process and the role of the audience in shaping the meaning of a performance.

In conclusion, the definition and evolution of performance art are rooted in experimentation, boundary-breaking, and audience engagement. As students of Performance Studies, it is essential to explore the rich history of performance art and its contemporary manifestations. By delving into this subchapter, you will gain invaluable insights into the transformative power of performance art and its relevance in our ever-changing world.

Understanding the Importance of Performance Art Studies

Performance art is a dynamic and captivating art form that has the power to engage, challenge, and inspire audiences. It encompasses a wide range of creative expressions, including theater, dance, music, and more. As students of performance studies, it is essential to understand the importance of delving into this field and exploring its various dimensions.

One of the key reasons why performance art studies are crucial is because they provide a unique platform for self-expression and self-discovery. Through performance, students can explore and communicate their thoughts, emotions, and ideas in a way that is both personal and universal. It allows them to develop their own artistic voice and gain a deeper understanding of themselves and the world around them.

Furthermore, performance art studies foster creativity and innovation. By exploring different techniques, styles, and genres, students are encouraged to think outside the box and push the boundaries of traditional artistic norms. This not only enhances their artistic abilities but also nurtures their ability to think critically, solve problems, and adapt to new challenges – skills that are highly valued in various professional fields.

Performance studies also promote collaboration and teamwork. In this field, artists often work in groups or ensembles, learning to trust and rely on one another. Through collaborative projects, students develop strong communication skills, learn to compromise, and appreciate diverse perspectives. These skills are not only vital for success in performance art but are also highly transferable to other areas of life, such as the workplace.

Moreover, studying performance art allows students to engage with different cultures, histories, and social issues. Performance has always been a powerful medium for social commentary and activism. By exploring the works of artists from various backgrounds and time periods, students gain a deeper understanding of the world's diversity and the challenges faced by different communities. This knowledge empowers them to use their art to create positive change and contribute to society.

In conclusion, performance art studies are of utmost importance for students interested in the field of performance studies. They offer a platform for self-expression, foster creativity, promote teamwork, and encourage social awareness. By mastering the art of performance, students not only develop their artistic abilities but also cultivate valuable life skills that will serve them well in their future endeavors.

Chapter 2: The Basics of Performance Art

Exploring Different Forms of Performance Art

Performance art is a versatile and ever-evolving field that offers a diverse range of artistic expressions. In this subchapter, we will delve into the captivating world of performance art and explore its various forms. Whether you are a student of performance studies or simply a curious individual seeking to expand your artistic horizons, this chapter will provide you with a comprehensive introduction to the different forms of performance art.

One of the most widely recognized forms of performance art is theater. From classical plays to avant-garde experimental productions, theater performances bring stories to life through the combined efforts of actors, directors, and designers. Theater offers a unique platform for exploring themes, emotions, and social issues, making it an essential part of performance studies.

Another form of performance art that has gained significant popularity in recent years is dance. From ballet to contemporary dance, this expressive art form combines movement, music, and storytelling to create captivating performances. Dance allows performers to convey emotions and narratives through their bodies, making it a visually stunning and emotionally evocative art form.

Performance art also includes disciplines such as performance poetry, where words are transformed into a dynamic and engaging experience for both performers and audiences. Performance poets use their voices, gestures, and body language to enhance the impact of their poems, creating a powerful connection with the audience.

In addition to these traditional forms, performance art has evolved to encompass various interdisciplinary and multimedia practices. Performance installations, for example, blur the boundaries between visual art, sculpture, and live performance. These immersive experiences often invite audience participation, encouraging them to engage with the artwork and become part of the performance itself.

Performance art is not limited to conventional art spaces either. Street performances, for instance, offer a vibrant and interactive form of art that takes place in public spaces. Street performers captivate passersby with their skills in music, dance, theater, and other forms of artistic expression, creating a unique and spontaneous experience.

As students of performance studies, it is crucial to explore and appreciate the diversity of performance art forms. By embracing various disciplines, we can broaden our understanding of what performance means and develop our own artistic voice. So, whether you find yourself drawn to the traditional stage or the uncharted territories of interdisciplinary performance, remember that there is no limit to the possibilities within the world of performance art.

Understanding the Role of the Performer

In the world of performance studies, the role of the performer is crucial and multifaceted. Whether you are an actor, musician, dancer, or any other type of performer, it is essential to understand the significance of your role and the impact it can have on both the audience and yourself. In this subchapter, we will explore the various aspects of the performer's role and how you can maximize your potential as a performer.

First and foremost, the performer serves as a conduit for the artistic expression. As a performer, you have the unique ability to bring a script, a musical composition, or a choreography to life. Your interpretation, emotions, and physicality breathe life into the work, making it relatable and engaging for the audience. It is important to remember that your role is not just about executing the technical aspects of your craft but also about connecting with the material and conveying its essence to the audience.

Furthermore, the performer acts as a storyteller. Whether you are performing in a theatre production, a concert, or a dance recital, you are essentially telling a story. Your job is to communicate the narrative, emotions, and themes of the performance through your body, voice, and expressions. By understanding the story you are telling and the message you want to convey, you can create a more impactful performance that resonates with the audience.

In addition to being a storyteller, the performer is also an interpreter. You have the power to bring your own unique perspective and interpretation to the work. This interpretation can be influenced by your personal experiences, emotions, and understanding of the material. By embracing your individuality and incorporating it into your performance, you can create a more authentic and compelling experience for both yourself and the audience.

Finally, the performer acts as a bridge between the audience and the art form. Your performance has the ability to connect with the audience on an emotional and intellectual level. It can transport them to different worlds, evoke empathy, and provoke thought. By understanding the needs and expectations of the audience, you can tailor your performance to create a meaningful and memorable experience for them.

In conclusion, understanding the role of the performer in the context of performance studies is essential for any student aspiring to master the art of performance. By recognizing yourself as a conduit, storyteller, interpreter, and bridge, you can unlock your full potential as a performer. Embrace your role with passion, dedication, and authenticity, and you will be able to create performances that leave a lasting impact on both yourself and your audience.

Chapter 3: Preparing for a Performance

Setting Goals and Objectives for Your Performance

In the world of performance studies, it is crucial for students to set clear goals and objectives to achieve success. Whether you are a dancer, actor, musician, or any other type of performer, having a clear direction can greatly enhance your skills and help you grow as an artist. This subchapter will guide you through the process of setting goals and objectives for your performance, providing you with a roadmap to excel in your craft.

First and foremost, it is important to understand the difference between goals and objectives. Goals are the broad, long-term aspirations you have for your performance. They provide you with a sense of purpose and serve as a vision for your artistic journey. Objectives, on the other hand, are the specific, measurable steps you take to reach your goals. They act as milestones along the way, ensuring that you are making progress and staying on track.

When setting goals, it is crucial to make them realistic, yet challenging. Set goals that align with your capabilities and current level of expertise, but also push you beyond your comfort zone. This will motivate you to continuously improve and strive for excellence. Additionally, goals should be specific and measurable. For example, rather than setting a vague goal like "improve my acting skills," specify a measurable objective such as "learn to effectively portray emotions through physical gestures."

To effectively set objectives, break down your goals into smaller, manageable tasks. This will make them less overwhelming and more attainable. For instance, if your goal is to become a proficient pianist, your objectives could include practicing scales for 30 minutes each day, learning a new piece every two weeks, or participating in a local piano competition. By breaking down your goals into smaller tasks, you can monitor your progress and stay motivated.

Furthermore, it is important to periodically evaluate your goals and objectives. As you progress in your performance studies, your aspirations may change, and new opportunities may arise. Regularly reassessing your goals will ensure they remain relevant and align with your evolving artistic journey.

Setting goals and objectives is not just about achieving success; it is also about personal growth and fulfillment. By having a clear direction and a well-defined plan, you will not only become a better performer but also gain a deeper understanding of yourself as an artist. So, take the time to set your goals and objectives, and embark on a journey of mastering the art of performance.

Developing a Concept and Theme

In the world of performance studies, one of the most crucial steps in creating a successful and impactful performance is developing a concept and theme. This subchapter of "Mastering the Art of Performance: A Student's Perspective" aims to guide students through the process of brainstorming, refining, and ultimately choosing a concept and theme that will captivate their audience.

When starting this creative journey, it is essential to understand that a concept and theme serve as the foundation for your performance. They provide a framework that will guide your artistic choices, from selecting music and costumes to choreography and staging. Therefore, it is essential to choose a concept and theme that resonates with you and can be effectively communicated to your audience.

The first step in developing a concept and theme is introspection. Take the time to reflect on your personal experiences, passions, and interests. What stories do you want to tell? What emotions do you want to evoke? By delving deep into your own experiences, you can uncover unique and authentic ideas that will set your performance apart.

Once you have a few ideas in mind, it's time to refine them. Research existing performances and explore different artistic forms to gain inspiration and broaden your understanding of what is possible. Experiment with visualizations, sketches, or even small-scale performances to see how your concept and theme translate into the performance space.

Throughout this process, consider the audience you are targeting. What will resonate with them? What message do you want to convey? Remember, your performance should not only entertain but also provoke thought and evoke emotions in your viewers.

As you refine your ideas, seek feedback from peers, mentors, and even potential audience members. Their insights can help you identify strengths and weaknesses in your concept and theme, allowing you to make necessary adjustments and improvements.

Finally, choose the concept and theme that aligns most closely with your artistic vision and resonates with your audience. Once you have made your choice, it's time to dive into the details and start bringing your performance to life.

In conclusion, developing a concept and theme is a crucial step in the creation of any performance. By delving into your personal experiences, refining your ideas, and seeking feedback, you can ensure that your concept and theme will captivate your audience and create a memorable experience. So, embrace your creativity, trust your instincts, and let your concept and theme guide you on a transformative artistic journey.

Creating a Performance Plan

In the exciting world of performance studies, mastering the art of performance requires more than just talent and passion. It demands careful planning and preparation to ensure success on stage. Whether you're an aspiring actor, dancer, musician, or any other type of performer, having a performance plan in place will guide you towards achieving your goals and reaching your fullest potential. This subchapter will provide you with valuable insights and practical tips on how to create a performance plan that will set you up for success.

1. Define Your Goals: The first step in creating a performance plan is to clearly define your goals. Ask yourself what you want to achieve with your performance. Do you aim to improve your skills, gain more experience, or land a specific role? By setting clear and achievable goals, you will have a clear direction and motivation to work towards.

2. Assess Your Abilities: Take an honest look at your current abilities and identify areas that require improvement. This self-assessment will help you prioritize your practice sessions and focus on areas that need the most attention. Seek feedback from mentors or instructors to gain an outside perspective on your strengths and weaknesses.

3. Set a Schedule: Time management is crucial when it comes to creating a performance plan. Set aside dedicated practice and rehearsal times in your schedule. Consistency is key, so aim for regular practice sessions rather than sporadic bursts of effort. Break down tasks into smaller, manageable chunks to make progress more attainable.

4. Create a Practice Routine: Design a practice routine that aligns with your goals and schedule. Focus on both technical skills and artistic

expression. Incorporate warm-up exercises, drills, and rehearsal techniques that target specific areas of improvement. Practice regularly and with intention to refine your performance.

5. Seek Feedback and Collaborate: Collaborating with others and seeking feedback are essential aspects of performance studies. Engage with fellow performers, instructors, and mentors who can provide valuable insights and constructive criticism. Embrace feedback as an opportunity for growth and improvement.

6. Reflect and Adjust: Regularly evaluate your progress and reflect on your performances. Identify what worked well and areas that need improvement. Adjust your performance plan accordingly to address any weaknesses or new goals that arise.

By creating a performance plan, you are taking control of your artistic journey and setting yourself up for success in the field of performance studies. Remember, the process is just as important as the final outcome. Embrace the challenge, stay committed, and enjoy the journey towards mastering the art of performance.

Chapter 4: The Importance of Rehearsal

Establishing a Rehearsal Schedule

One of the most crucial aspects of mastering the art of performance is establishing and maintaining a well-structured rehearsal schedule. As students in the field of performance studies, we understand the importance of discipline and dedication in honing our skills and delivering outstanding performances. In this subchapter, we will delve into the strategies and guidelines for creating an effective rehearsal schedule that will maximize our potential.

A rehearsal schedule serves as the backbone of any successful performance. It provides structure, organization, and helps us manage our time effectively. The first step in establishing a rehearsal schedule is setting clear goals and objectives. By defining the specific areas we want to focus on, whether it be vocal techniques, physical movements, or emotional expression, we can allocate the appropriate amount of time to each aspect.

Once goals are established, it is important to create a realistic and manageable schedule. Take into consideration your other commitments such as classes, work, or personal obligations, and make sure to allocate sufficient time for rest and relaxation. Remember, a tired and burnt-out performer cannot deliver their best.

Consider the needs of your specific performance. Are you part of a group or performing a solo act? If you are part of a group, coordinate with your fellow performers to determine the best times for group rehearsals. This collaboration will ensure that everyone is on the same page and can practice together effectively.

Furthermore, it is essential to establish a consistent routine. Consistency helps to build discipline and allows us to develop muscle memory, making our performances more natural and effortless. Determine the best times of day for rehearsals, taking into account when you feel most energized and focused.

In addition to regular rehearsals, it is also beneficial to incorporate individual practice sessions into your schedule. These sessions allow you to focus on personal growth and improvement, addressing specific areas that require extra attention.

Lastly, flexibility is key. Rehearsal schedules may need to be adjusted from time to time due to unforeseen circumstances or changes in the performance requirements. Be open to adapt and make necessary adjustments without losing sight of your goals.

By establishing a rehearsal schedule that is well-structured, realistic, and adaptable, we can truly master the art of performance. Remember, success in performance studies is not achieved overnight, but through consistent effort and dedication. So, let's take ownership of our craft, create a rehearsal schedule that works for us, and watch our performances soar to new heights.

Techniques for Effective Rehearsals

Rehearsals are an essential part of any performance, allowing us to refine our skills, polish our technique, and achieve a seamless and captivating performance. In this subchapter, we will explore some techniques for effective rehearsals that will help students in the niche of performance studies master the art of performance.

First and foremost, it is crucial to establish a structured rehearsal plan. Begin by breaking down the performance into smaller sections or scenes and allocate specific time slots for each. This will ensure that you cover all aspects of the performance and allow for focused practice. Additionally, set clear goals for each rehearsal, whether it is perfecting a particular dance routine, improving vocal projection, or mastering a challenging monologue. By setting specific objectives, you can measure your progress and stay motivated throughout the rehearsal process.

Another technique for effective rehearsals is to create a supportive and collaborative environment. Encourage open communication and feedback among team members, as this will foster a sense of unity and enable everyone to contribute their ideas and insights. Remember, rehearsals are not just about individual growth but also about working together as a cohesive unit to deliver a stellar performance.

Furthermore, incorporating visualization exercises can significantly enhance your rehearsal experience. Take a few moments at the beginning of each rehearsal to visualize yourself performing flawlessly. Imagine the audience's positive reaction, the applause, and the sense of accomplishment. This technique will not only boost your confidence but also help you mentally prepare for the actual performance.

Additionally, exploring different rehearsal techniques such as running scenes in slow motion, experimenting with various blocking options, or improvising certain sections can inject creativity and freshness into your performance. These techniques will allow you to discover new possibilities, develop your character, and add depth to your interpretation.

Finally, never underestimate the power of repetition. Practice makes perfect, and the more you repeat certain movements, lines, or musical phrases, the more natural and effortless they will become. Repetition also helps build muscle memory, ensuring that you can perform with confidence and precision.

In conclusion, effective rehearsals are the building blocks of a successful performance. By implementing these techniques and strategies, students in the niche of performance studies can master the art of performance. Remember to plan your rehearsals, create a supportive environment, visualize success, explore different techniques, and embrace the power of repetition. With dedication, perseverance, and a commitment to continuous improvement, you will undoubtedly take your performance skills to new heights. Keep practicing, and break a leg!

Overcoming Challenges during Rehearsal

Rehearsals play a crucial role in the journey of every performer, offering a platform to refine their skills and bring their best to the stage. However, the process is not without its challenges. In this subchapter, we will explore some of the common obstacles that students studying performance studies may face during rehearsals and provide strategies to overcome them.

One of the significant challenges during rehearsals is the fear of making mistakes. It is essential to remember that mistakes are a natural part of the learning process. Embrace them as valuable opportunities to grow and improve. By creating a supportive and non-judgmental environment within the rehearsal space, students can feel more comfortable taking risks and pushing their boundaries.

Time management is another hurdle that students often encounter. Balancing rehearsals with other academic commitments can be demanding, leading to stress and exhaustion. To overcome this challenge, it is crucial to prioritize and plan ahead. Set realistic goals and create a schedule that allows for sufficient rest and preparation. Breaking tasks into smaller, manageable chunks can also help in utilizing time effectively.

Communication breakdowns can hinder the progress of a rehearsal. Misunderstandings, lack of clarity, or ego clashes can disrupt the harmony within the group. To address this challenge, fostering open and honest communication is vital. Encourage active listening, clear articulation of ideas, and respect for everyone's opinions. When conflicts arise, approach them with a problem-solving mindset, seeking compromise and common ground.

Technical difficulties can pose a significant challenge during rehearsals, such as issues with sound equipment or lighting. It is essential to be proactive in finding solutions to technical problems. Develop a basic understanding of the technical aspects involved in your performance and communicate any issues promptly to the relevant personnel. Additionally, having a backup plan or alternative arrangements can help overcome unexpected technical glitches.

Lastly, maintaining motivation and focus throughout the rehearsal process can be demanding, particularly during long and intensive sessions. To combat this challenge, set personal goals and remind yourself of the bigger picture. Surround yourself with supportive peers who share your passion for performance. Celebrate small victories along the way, and remember that perseverance is key to overcoming any obstacles.

In conclusion, rehearsals are an integral part of mastering the art of performance. By acknowledging and addressing the challenges that may arise, students studying performance studies can navigate through them with confidence and resilience. Embrace mistakes, manage time effectively, foster open communication, find technical solutions, and stay motivated. With these strategies, students can transform challenges into opportunities for growth and ultimately deliver outstanding performances.

Chapter 5: Enhancing Stage Presence

Building Confidence as a Performer

Confidence is an essential quality for any performer in the field of Performance Studies. Whether you are an aspiring actor, dancer, musician, or public speaker, developing self-assurance is crucial to excel in your chosen path. In this subchapter, we will explore various strategies and techniques that will help you build confidence as a performer.

One of the first steps in building confidence is to acknowledge and embrace your strengths. Every performer has unique talents, skills, and qualities that set them apart. Take the time to reflect on what makes you an exceptional performer and focus on nurturing those aspects. By recognizing and appreciating your abilities, you will naturally gain confidence in your own capabilities.

Another valuable technique is to practice regularly and consistently. As the saying goes, "practice makes perfect." The more you practice, the more familiar and comfortable you become with your material or routine. This familiarity breeds confidence and allows you to deliver your performance with ease and poise. Additionally, consistent practice helps you overcome any stage fright or nervousness that may hinder your confidence.

Furthermore, seeking constructive feedback and guidance from mentors and peers can greatly boost your confidence as a performer. Constructive criticism allows you to identify areas for improvement and refine your skills. Accepting feedback gracefully and using it to grow not only enhances your abilities but also instills a sense of confidence in your progress.

Visualization is another powerful tool to build confidence. Before a performance, take a few moments to visualize yourself succeeding and captivating your audience. Imagine the applause, the standing ovation, and the feeling of accomplishment. This positive visualization primes your mind for success and instills confidence in your abilities.

Lastly, remember to maintain a positive mindset. Self-doubt can be detrimental to your confidence as a performer. Instead, focus on positive affirmations and surround yourself with supportive individuals who believe in your talent. By cultivating a positive mental attitude, you will radiate confidence and charisma on stage.

In conclusion, building confidence as a performer is a lifelong journey. It requires self-reflection, practice, seeking feedback, visualization, and a positive mindset. By implementing these strategies and techniques, you can steadily enhance your confidence and become a truly captivating performer. Remember, confidence is not only the key to success but also the key to enjoying and embracing the art of performance.

Techniques for Captivating an Audience

In the world of performance studies, captivating an audience is an essential skill that can make or break a performance. Whether you are a musician, actor, dancer, or public speaker, the ability to engage and mesmerize your audience is what sets you apart from the rest. In this subchapter, we will explore some tried and tested techniques that will help you master the art of captivating an audience.

1. Know your audience: Before stepping on stage, take the time to research and understand your audience. What are their interests? What do they expect from your performance? By tailoring your act to their preferences, you can create a connection that will keep them engaged throughout.

2. Use storytelling: Humans are wired to respond to stories. Incorporating storytelling techniques into your performance can help create an emotional connection with your audience. Whether it's through lyrics, monologues, or dance movements, storytelling adds depth and relatability to your performance.

3. Utilize body language: Your body speaks volumes on stage. Use your posture, facial expressions, and gestures to convey the emotions and messages of your performance. A confident and expressive body language will draw your audience's attention and keep them engaged.

4. Create moments of surprise: Surprise your audience with unexpected moments. Add a twist in your performance, introduce a sudden change in tempo, or incorporate a surprising prop. These unexpected elements will grab your audience's attention and leave a lasting impression.

5. Interact with your audience: Engaging with your audience during your performance can create a sense of connection and involvement. Make eye contact, acknowledge applause or laughter, and even invite participation when appropriate. This interaction will make your audience feel like a part of the performance, enhancing their engagement.

6. Use visual aids and technology: Visual aids and technology can enhance your performance and captivate your audience. Utilize lighting, projection, or multimedia elements to create a visually stunning experience. However, make sure these elements complement your performance rather than overshadow it.

7. Practice, practice, practice: The key to captivating an audience is honing your skills through relentless practice. Rehearse your performance until it becomes second nature. This will give you the confidence and freedom to truly connect with your audience, leaving no room for nerves or self-doubt.

Remember, captivating an audience is an art that requires constant refinement. By implementing these techniques and continuously exploring new ways to engage your audience, you will become a master of performance. Embrace the challenge, unleash your creativity, and make your mark on the stage!

Utilizing Body Language and Facial Expressions

In the world of performance studies, mastering the art of communication goes beyond words. Body language and facial expressions play a crucial role in conveying emotions, intentions, and connecting with an audience. Whether you are a dancer, actor, musician, or any other performer, understanding and utilizing these non-verbal cues can elevate your performance to new heights.

Body language encompasses the movements, gestures, and postures we use to express ourselves. Every motion we make on stage carries meaning and can either enhance or detract from our performance. By consciously controlling and manipulating our body language, we can effectively communicate our character's emotions, thoughts, and motivations. For example, a slouched posture might convey sadness or defeat, while a confident stance can project strength and authority. It is crucial for students of performance studies to explore and experiment with different body movements to find the ones that best align with their characters and performances.

Facial expressions, on the other hand, are windows to our soul. Our face is an incredibly expressive canvas, capable of conveying a wide range of emotions. The way we use our eyes, eyebrows, mouth, and other facial features can bring a character to life and elicit powerful responses from the audience. A simple smile can communicate joy, while a furrowed brow might indicate confusion or concern. Students must learn how to control and manipulate their facial expressions to accurately convey the intended emotions and effectively communicate with their audience.

To master the art of utilizing body language and facial expressions, students must first develop a deep understanding of their characters and the emotions they wish to evoke. This requires extensive research, observation, and introspection. By immersing themselves in their character's world, students can tap into their own emotions and experiences, allowing them to authentically express themselves on stage.

Furthermore, students should also pay attention to the body language and facial expressions of others, both in everyday life and in performances. By observing how people naturally express themselves, students can gain valuable insights and inspiration for their own performances.

In conclusion, mastering the art of performance requires a thorough understanding and effective utilization of body language and facial expressions. By consciously controlling and manipulating these non-verbal cues, students in the field of performance studies can effectively communicate their characters' emotions, thoughts, and motivations, leaving a lasting impact on their audience. Through practice, observation, and dedication, students can unlock the full potential of their performances and truly master the art of communication on stage.

Chapter 6: Exploring Voice and Movement

Developing Vocal Techniques for Performance

In the world of performance studies, mastering vocal techniques is essential for any aspiring artist. Your voice is an incredibly powerful instrument, capable of conveying emotions, telling stories, and captivating an audience. Whether you dream of becoming a singer, an actor, or a public speaker, honing your vocal skills will undoubtedly enhance your overall performance.

This subchapter aims to provide students with valuable insights and practical exercises to develop their vocal techniques for performance. From breathing exercises to vocal warm-ups, we will explore various aspects that will help you unlock the full potential of your voice.

One of the fundamental aspects of vocal technique is proper breath control. Learning how to breathe deeply and diaphragmatically is crucial for projecting your voice and sustaining long notes. We will walk you through different breathing exercises and techniques that will strengthen your breath support, allowing you to deliver powerful performances on stage.

Another vital aspect we will delve into is vocal warm-ups. Just like athletes warm up before a game, vocal warm-ups are essential to prepare your voice for performance. We will introduce you to a range of vocal exercises that will not only warm up your vocal cords but also improve your vocal range, flexibility, and resonance. These exercises will help you find your unique vocal style and develop a strong and versatile voice.

Furthermore, we will explore the importance of diction and articulation in performance. Clear and precise diction enables the audience to understand every word you say or sing, ensuring effective communication of your message. We will provide tips and exercises to improve your diction and articulation, allowing you to enunciate words with clarity and precision.

Lastly, we will touch upon the significance of stage presence and connecting with your audience. Developing confidence and charisma on stage is essential for leaving a lasting impression. We will offer practical advice on how to engage your audience through body language, eye contact, and vocal expression, creating a captivating and memorable performance.

By mastering the vocal techniques discussed in this subchapter, you will develop a strong foundation for your performance career. Remember, practice is key. Regularly incorporating these techniques into your routine will lead to improvements in your vocal abilities and enhance your overall performance skills.

So, let's embark on this vocal journey together and unleash the full potential of your voice in the world of performance studies. Get ready to captivate your audience with your newfound vocal prowess and leave a lasting impact on stage.

Understanding the Power of Body Language

In the world of performance studies, mastering the art of communication is critical. While verbal communication often takes the spotlight, one must not underestimate the power of body language. It is said that actions speak louder than words, and this is particularly true in the realm of performance. In this subchapter, we will delve into the significance of body language and its impact on performance, providing students with valuable insights on how to harness this power.

Body language encompasses all the non-verbal cues we send out through our posture, gestures, facial expressions, and even our breathing. It is a language of its own, capable of conveying emotions, intentions, and messages without uttering a single word. As students in the field of performance studies, understanding and utilizing body language effectively can greatly enhance your ability to captivate an audience and deliver a compelling performance.

One of the key aspects to grasp is the correlation between body language and emotional expression. Our bodies have a natural tendency to reflect our internal states. By consciously controlling our body language, we can manipulate our emotions and convey them to the audience. For instance, a slouched posture might convey a lack of confidence, while an upright posture exudes authority and self-assuredness. Such subtle cues can significantly impact how your performance is received.

Moreover, body language plays a crucial role in establishing connections with the audience. Eye contact, for example, is a powerful tool for building rapport. By making direct eye contact with individuals in the audience, you can create a sense of intimacy and engagement. Similarly, open and inviting gestures can help establish a connection, while closed-off or defensive postures can create a barrier between you and the audience.

Understanding the power of body language also involves being aware of cultural nuances. Different cultures have distinct norms and interpretations of body language. Therefore, it is important to adapt your non-verbal cues accordingly when performing in diverse settings. This knowledge allows you to effectively communicate and connect with audiences from various backgrounds.

In conclusion, body language is an integral part of performance studies. By understanding its significance and harnessing its power, students can take their performances to new heights. Remember, your body speaks volumes even before you utter a single word. Mastering the art of body language will not only enhance your performances but also enable you to connect with audiences on a deeper level. So, embrace the power of body language and let your movements speak for themselves.

Incorporating Dance and Movement in Performance

As students of Performance Studies, we have the unique opportunity to explore various art forms and techniques that enhance our abilities as performers. One such technique that holds immense power in captivating an audience is the incorporation of dance and movement in our performances. In this subchapter, we will delve into the importance of dance and movement, and how we can effectively incorporate them into our own performances.

Dance and movement have been integral parts of performance art for centuries. From classical ballet to contemporary dance forms, movement has always played a significant role in conveying emotions, stories, and ideas. As performers, it is crucial to understand the impact that movement can have on our audience. It allows us to communicate in a way that words alone cannot, creating a visual language that resonates deeply with viewers.

When incorporating dance and movement into our performances, it is essential to consider the context and purpose of our piece. Whether it is a theatrical production, a dance performance, or a multimedia presentation, each genre requires a unique approach to movement. By analyzing the themes, characters, and overall message of our performance, we can make informed decisions about the types of movements that will best convey our intentions.

One key aspect of incorporating dance and movement is the development of physicality. This involves understanding our bodies and their capabilities, and training them to execute movements with precision and grace. Through regular physical training, we can improve our strength, flexibility, and coordination, enabling us to perform even the most complex choreography with ease.

Furthermore, dance and movement can be used as powerful tools for storytelling. By choreographing movements that represent the emotions and actions of our characters, we can create a narrative that is both visually captivating and emotionally engaging. This allows us to connect with our audience on a deeper level, eliciting a range of emotions and leaving a lasting impression.

In conclusion, incorporating dance and movement into our performances is a valuable technique that can elevate our artistry as performers. By understanding the significance of movement, developing our physicality, and utilizing choreography to tell stories, we can create performances that are truly unforgettable. As students of Performance Studies, let us embrace the power of dance and movement, and continue to push the boundaries of our artistic expression.

Chapter 7: Improvisation in Performance Art

Embracing Spontaneity and Creativity

In the exhilarating world of performance studies, the ability to embrace spontaneity and creativity can truly elevate your craft. As students delving into this exciting field, it is crucial to understand the immense value of these qualities and how they can contribute to your growth and success as an artist.

When we think of performance, we often associate it with meticulous planning and rehearsed routines. While structure and preparation are undoubtedly important, it is the moments of spontaneity that add a touch of magic to any performance. Embracing spontaneity allows you to be present in the moment, respond to unexpected situations, and connect with your audience on a deeper level. It enables you to tap into your instincts and unleash your authentic self, bringing a fresh and unique perspective to your work.

Creativity, on the other hand, fuels innovation and pushes boundaries. It is the driving force behind groundbreaking performances that leave a lasting impact. As students, it is crucial to nurture and cultivate your creative spirits. Allow yourself to think outside the box, explore new ideas, and experiment with different techniques. Embrace the freedom to take risks and challenge conventional norms. Remember, it is through creativity that you will discover your true artistic voice and develop a signature style that sets you apart from the rest.

So how can you foster spontaneity and creativity within your performance studies journey? Firstly, be open to new experiences and constantly seek inspiration from various sources. Attend performances, read books, watch films, and engage in conversations with fellow artists. Surround yourself with individuals who encourage and nurture your creativity. Collaboration is a powerful tool that can spark innovative ideas and lead to extraordinary performances.

Additionally, practice improvisation regularly. This will not only enhance your ability to think on your feet but also strengthen your creative muscles. Improvisation exercises help you trust your instincts, break free from self-doubt, and embrace the unknown. Remember, the more comfortable you become with spontaneity, the more it will become an integral part of your artistic process.

In conclusion, embracing spontaneity and creativity is vital for students in the field of performance studies. These qualities allow you to bring a fresh perspective to your work, connect deeply with your audience, and develop a unique artistic voice. So, let go of fear, take risks, and embrace the joy of spontaneity and creativity. Unleash your inner artist and watch as your performances soar to new heights.

Improvisation Techniques and Exercises

Improvisation is a vital skill in the world of performance studies, allowing actors, musicians, and dancers to think on their feet, adapt to unexpected situations, and create in the moment. This subchapter explores various techniques and exercises that can help students master the art of improvisation and enhance their performance abilities.

1. Introduction to Improvisation: Before diving into the techniques and exercises, it is essential to understand the concept of improvisation. Students will learn the importance of being present, listening to their fellow performers, and embracing spontaneity.

2. Building Trust and Collaboration: Successful improvisation relies heavily on trust and collaboration among performers. This section introduces exercises designed to foster trust, enhance communication, and encourage teamwork. Students will engage in partner exercises, group activities, and trust-building games to establish a strong foundation for improvisation.

3. Yes, And...: The "Yes, And..." technique is a fundamental principle in improvisation. Students will learn to accept and build upon the ideas presented by their fellow performers, rather than rejecting or blocking them. Through interactive exercises, students will practice saying "yes" to offers, expanding upon them, and creating cohesive scenes or musical pieces.

4.   Character   Development:

Creating and developing compelling characters on the spot is crucial for improvisational success. This section introduces exercises that encourage students to explore physicality, vocal expression, and emotional depth to bring their characters to life. Students will learn to make bold choices, adapt their characters to different scenarios, and maintain consistency throughout their performances.

5.   Improvisation   Games:

This section presents a collection of popular improvisation games that students can use for practice and performance. Games like "Freeze," "Props," and "Sound Ball" challenge students to think quickly, make split-second decisions, and interact seamlessly with their fellow performers.

6.   Musical   Improvisation:

For students interested in performance studies within the realm of music, this section offers exercises and techniques specific to musical improvisation. Students will learn to improvise melodies, harmonies, and rhythms, as well as explore various genres and styles.

Conclusion:

Improvisation is a valuable skill that not only enhances performance abilities but also fosters creativity, adaptability, and spontaneity. By incorporating the techniques and exercises explored in this subchapter, students will gain confidence in their ability to think on their feet, collaborate effectively, and deliver captivating performances.

Whether students are aspiring actors, musicians, or dancers, the mastery of improvisation techniques will undoubtedly enrich their performance studies and open doors to exciting opportunities in the world of performing arts.

Challenges and Benefits of Improvisation

In the world of performance studies, improvisation holds a special place as a skill that can both challenge and benefit students. Whether you are an actor, musician, dancer, or any other kind of performer, the ability to improvise can greatly enhance your artistry and open up new possibilities in your performances. However, it is not without its challenges.

One of the main challenges of improvisation is the fear of the unknown. Improvising requires stepping out of your comfort zone and trusting your instincts in the moment. It can be intimidating to let go of pre-planned routines and embrace the uncertainty of the present. Additionally, improvisation requires quick thinking and adaptability, which can be mentally and physically demanding. It takes practice and experience to develop the confidence and fluidity needed to improvise effectively.

Despite these challenges, the benefits of improvisation are numerous and transformative. Firstly, improvisation allows performers to truly connect with their art and express their unique voice. It encourages individuality and creativity, as there are no prescribed rules or limitations. Through improvisation, students can discover new ways of interpreting and presenting their work, leading to groundbreaking performances that resonate with audiences.

Moreover, improvisation hones vital skills for performers, such as active listening and collaboration. In improvisational settings, performers must be fully present and attuned to their fellow performers, responding to their cues and building upon their ideas.

This fosters a sense of unity and trust within the group, as performers learn to rely on each other and create together in real-time.

Furthermore, improvisation strengthens problem-solving abilities by forcing performers to think on their feet and find solutions in the moment. This skill is not only valuable on stage but also in everyday life, as it enhances adaptability and resilience in the face of unexpected challenges.

In conclusion, the challenges and benefits of improvisation in the realm of performance studies are intertwined. While it can be daunting, embracing improvisation as a student can lead to personal and artistic growth. It is an opportunity to push boundaries, discover new artistic territories, and develop essential skills that will serve you both on and off the stage. So, take a leap into the unknown and see where your improvisational journey takes you – the possibilities are endless!

Chapter 8: Dealing with Stage Fright and Performance Anxiety

Recognizing the Causes of Stage Fright

Stage fright is a common phenomenon that many performers experience before stepping onto the stage. It can be an overwhelming feeling of anxiety and fear that can hinder one's ability to deliver a successful performance. However, understanding the root causes of stage fright can help students in the field of performance studies overcome this fear and master the art of performance.

One of the main causes of stage fright is the fear of judgment and criticism from others. As students, we often worry about what our peers or instructors will think of our performance. This fear of being negatively evaluated can create a sense of pressure and self-doubt, ultimately leading to stage fright. To overcome this, it is important to remember that constructive criticism is a valuable part of the learning process. Instead of fearing judgment, view it as an opportunity for growth and improvement.

Another cause of stage fright is a lack of self-confidence. Students may doubt their abilities and worry about making mistakes or forgetting their lines. This self-doubt can be paralyzing and prevent performers from showcasing their true potential on stage. Building self-confidence is crucial to overcoming stage fright. Practice regularly, know your material inside out, and remind yourself of your accomplishments and strengths as a performer. Embrace positive self-talk and visualize success on stage to boost your confidence.

The fear of failure is also a common cause of stage fright. Students may fear making mistakes or experiencing technical difficulties during their performance. It is important to remember that mistakes are a natural part of the learning process. Instead of dwelling on the fear of failure, focus on the joy of performing and the opportunity to share your passion with others. Embrace a growth mindset, where mistakes are seen as stepping stones towards improvement.

Lastly, the physical symptoms of stage fright, such as trembling, sweating, and a racing heartbeat, can intensify the fear and anxiety. Understanding that these symptoms are normal physiological responses to stress can help alleviate some of the anxiety. Breathing exercises, meditation, and physical warm-ups can help calm the nerves and prepare the body for performance.

In conclusion, recognizing the causes of stage fright is the first step towards overcoming it. By understanding and addressing the fear of judgment, lack of self-confidence, fear of failure, and the physical symptoms associated with stage fright, students in the field of performance studies can develop strategies to conquer this common fear. With practice, perseverance, and a positive mindset, students can master the art of performance and deliver captivating and confident performances on stage.

Coping Strategies for Overcoming Stage Fright

Introduction:
Stage fright is a common phenomenon that affects many students pursuing performance studies. The fear of performing in front of an audience can be paralyzing, causing anxiety, nervousness, and self-doubt. However, with the right coping strategies, you can overcome stage fright and achieve success in your performances. In this subchapter, we will explore effective techniques to help you conquer stage fright and enhance your overall performance skills.

1. Preparation is Key:
One of the most effective ways to combat stage fright is through thorough preparation. Rehearse your performance piece extensively, becoming familiar with every aspect, from script or music to choreography. The more prepared you are, the more confident you will feel on stage, reducing anxiety and fear.

2. Visualization and Positive Affirmations:
Visualizing success and using positive affirmations can significantly impact your stage performance. Close your eyes and imagine yourself delivering a flawless performance, receiving applause and praise. Repeat positive statements such as "I am confident," "I am talented," and "I can do this." These techniques help build self-belief and reduce anxiety.

3. Breathing and Relaxation Techniques:
Learning relaxation techniques and deep breathing exercises can help calm your nerves before going on stage. Practice deep belly breathing, inhaling slowly through your nose and exhaling through your mouth.

This helps regulate your heart rate and relax your muscles, reducing tension and anxiety.

4.   Focus   on   the   Present   Moment: Often, stage fright stems from worrying about what could go wrong or how the audience will perceive you. Instead, focus on the present moment and the joy of performing. Concentrate on your movements, lines, or music, and immerse yourself in the artistic experience. This shift in focus will help alleviate anxiety and enhance your overall enjoyment of the performance.

5.   Supportive   Environment: Seek support from fellow students, mentors, or teachers who understand your struggles and can provide guidance and encouragement. Surround yourself with positive individuals who believe in your abilities and can help boost your confidence. Building a supportive network can significantly reduce stage fright and enhance your performance experience.

Conclusion:
Stage fright is a common challenge faced by students in the field of performance studies. However, with the right coping strategies, you can overcome this fear and thrive on stage. Remember to prepare thoroughly, visualize success, practice relaxation techniques, focus on the present moment, and seek support from a supportive network. By implementing these strategies, you will gradually build confidence, conquer stage fright, and master the art of performance.

Building Resilience and Confidence

In the world of performance studies, resilience and confidence are two essential qualities that every student must cultivate. Whether you are an aspiring actor, dancer, musician, or any other performer, mastering these skills will not only enhance your artistic abilities but also contribute to your overall personal growth. This subchapter aims to guide students in building resilience and confidence, providing them with valuable tools to navigate the demanding world of performance.

Resilience is the ability to bounce back from setbacks and face challenges with determination and flexibility. As students in the field of performance, you will inevitably encounter obstacles, such as rejection, criticism, or performance anxiety. However, it is crucial to understand that these setbacks are not failures but opportunities for growth. By reframing your mindset and viewing setbacks as learning experiences, you can build resilience and continue striving for excellence.

One effective way to build resilience is through self-reflection. Take time to assess your strengths and weaknesses objectively. Identify areas for improvement and set realistic goals to work towards. Additionally, cultivating a support network of peers, mentors, and teachers can provide encouragement and guidance during difficult times. Surrounding yourself with like-minded individuals who understand the challenges of performance studies can help you stay motivated and resilient.

Confidence is another key attribute that every performer must develop. It is the belief in your own abilities and worth, which directly influences your stage presence and performance quality. Building confidence requires a combination of self-awareness and continued practice. Start by acknowledging your unique talents and strengths, and embrace them as part of your identity as a performer. Celebrate your achievements, no matter how small, and use them as stepping stones towards greater success.

To enhance confidence, consistent practice is vital. Regularly rehearsing and honing your skills will not only improve your technical abilities but also instill a sense of confidence in your performance. Remember, confidence is not about being flawless but about embracing imperfections and using them to connect with your audience authentically.

Lastly, maintaining a healthy mindset and self-care routine is crucial in building both resilience and confidence. Prioritize your physical and mental well-being by practicing relaxation techniques, such as meditation or breathing exercises. Additionally, engage in activities outside of your performance studies that bring you joy and fulfillment. Taking care of your overall well-being will contribute to your confidence and resilience in the long run.

By focusing on building resilience and confidence, students in the field of performance studies can navigate the challenges and uncertainties of their artistic journey. Remember, resilience is the fuel that keeps you going, and confidence is the spark that ignites your performance. Embrace these qualities, and let them guide you towards mastering the art of performance.

Chapter 9: Collaborative Performance Art

The Benefits and Challenges of Collaborative Work

Subchapter: The Benefits and Challenges of Collaborative Work

Collaboration is a fundamental aspect of the field of Performance Studies, and it offers a wide range of benefits and challenges for students. In this subchapter, we will explore how collaborative work can enhance your skills and knowledge while also discussing the potential hurdles you may encounter. Understanding these aspects will help you navigate the world of collaborative projects more effectively and achieve greater success in your academic journey.

Benefits of Collaborative Work:

1. Enhanced Creativity: Collaborating with fellow students allows you to tap into a diverse range of ideas, perspectives, and experiences. This exposure to different viewpoints can foster your creative thinking and inspire innovative approaches to performance projects.

2. Expanded Skill Set: Collaborative work often involves individuals with varied expertise. By working together, you have the opportunity to learn new skills and develop existing ones. For instance, if you excel in acting but struggle with set design, collaborating with a student who specializes in that area can help you expand your knowledge and abilities.

3. Increased Networking Opportunities: Collaborative projects provide an ideal platform to network with peers who share your passion for Performance Studies. Building connections within your field can lead

to future collaborations, job opportunities, and a broader support network throughout your career.

Challenges of Collaborative Work:

1. Communication Issues: Collaborative work requires effective communication to ensure everyone is on the same page. Differences in communication styles, misunderstandings, and conflicting schedules can pose challenges. However, learning to communicate openly, actively listen, and resolve conflicts will help overcome these obstacles.

2. Division of Labor: Assigning tasks and responsibilities can sometimes be a source of conflict within collaborative projects. It is crucial to establish clear roles and expectations from the beginning, ensuring that each member contributes equally and feels valued for their efforts.

3. Time Management: Collaborative work often involves coordinating schedules and meeting deadlines. Balancing multiple commitments can be challenging, but it provides an opportunity to develop essential time management skills, ensuring the completion of projects within stipulated timelines.

In conclusion, collaborative work in Performance Studies offers numerous benefits, including enhanced creativity, expanded skill sets, and increased networking opportunities. However, it also comes with challenges such as communication issues, division of labor, and time management. By understanding and addressing these challenges, you can make the most of collaborative projects and thrive in the field of Performance Studies.

Effective Communication and Conflict Resolution

In the realm of Performance Studies, effective communication and conflict resolution are paramount to achieving success and maintaining harmonious relationships. As students pursuing the art of performance, it is crucial to master these skills in order to excel in our chosen field. This subchapter aims to provide valuable insights and strategies to help students navigate the complexities of interpersonal dynamics, ensuring a positive and productive environment for artistic expression.

Communication lies at the heart of every successful performance, be it theater, dance, music, or any other form of artistic expression. As performers, we must learn to convey our ideas, emotions, and intentions effectively to our fellow artists and collaborators. This requires active listening, empathy, and the ability to articulate our thoughts clearly. By fostering an open and respectful communication environment, we can enhance our artistic collaborations and foster a strong sense of trust and camaraderie among the ensemble.

Conflict is an inevitable part of any creative process, but how we handle it determines the outcome. Conflict resolution skills are invaluable in navigating disagreements, differences of opinion, and artistic clashes. By developing effective conflict resolution strategies, we can transform conflicts into opportunities for growth and innovation. This involves active engagement with differing perspectives, seeking common ground, and finding creative solutions that satisfy everyone involved. Embracing conflict as a catalyst for improvement rather than a hindrance is a mindset shift that can greatly benefit our artistic endeavors.

To enhance our communication and conflict resolution skills, it is essential to cultivate self-awareness and emotional intelligence. Understanding our own strengths, weaknesses, and triggers enables us to communicate our needs and boundaries effectively. Additionally, by developing empathy and emotional intelligence, we can better understand the motivations and perspectives of others, leading to more fruitful collaborations and smoother conflict resolution processes.

Furthermore, incorporating effective communication and conflict resolution into our daily practice not only benefits our performance studies but also prepares us for life beyond the stage. These skills are transferable to various professional and personal contexts and will serve us well in all aspects of our lives.

Through mastering the art of effective communication and conflict resolution, we empower ourselves as performers and contribute to the growth and development of the Performance Studies field. By creating a positive and supportive environment, we foster creativity, collaboration, and innovation, enabling us to reach new heights in our artistic endeavors. Let us embrace these essential skills and embark on a journey of personal and artistic growth, as we strive to become masters of the art of performance.

Balancing Individual and Collective Expression

In the world of performance studies, there is a delicate balance between individual expression and collective collaboration. As students of this art, it is crucial to understand and navigate this dynamic in order to become successful performers. This subchapter aims to explore the significance of finding equilibrium between personal creativity and the demands of a collective performance.

Individual expression is at the core of every artist's journey. It is through our unique perspectives, emotions, and experiences that we find our voice as performers. As students, we must embrace this individuality and cultivate it through self-exploration and experimentation. By honing our strengths and understanding our weaknesses, we can develop a strong foundation from which to build upon.

However, it is essential to recognize that performance is not solely about the individual. It is about connecting with others, collaborating, and creating something greater than the sum of its parts. In a collective performance, every member has a role to play, and their contributions are integral to the success of the whole. This requires compromise, adaptability, and a willingness to put the needs of the group above personal desires.

Finding the balance between individual and collective expression is a continuous process. It involves active listening, open-mindedness, and effective communication within the group. It means respecting and valuing the ideas and perspectives of others while still staying true to our own artistic visions.

One way to achieve this balance is through improvisation. Improvisational exercises can help us develop the ability to respond in the moment, adapt to unexpected situations, and collaborate with others. By exploring different forms of improvisation, we can discover new ways to express ourselves while remaining connected to the collective experience.

Furthermore, studying diverse performance styles and techniques can expand our range as performers. By exploring different disciplines, such as theater, dance, music, or spoken word, we can gain a broader understanding of the possibilities within performance. This knowledge can enhance our individual expression while also enriching our collective performances.

In conclusion, mastering the art of performance requires finding a balance between individual and collective expression. As students, it is essential to nurture our individuality while also embracing collaboration and collective creativity. By actively engaging in self-reflection, open communication, and exploring various performance styles, we can find harmony between personal and collective artistic growth. It is through this delicate balance that we can truly excel in the world of performance studies.

Chapter 10: Performance Art Documentation

Understanding the Importance of Documentation

In the realm of performance studies, the significance of documentation cannot be emphasized enough. As students exploring the art of performance, it is crucial to recognize the immense value that documentation holds in preserving and showcasing our work. This subchapter aims to shed light on the importance of documentation and how it can enhance our understanding and growth as aspiring performers.

Documentation serves as a tangible record of our performances, capturing not only the final product but also the process that led to it. Through photographs, videos, written reflections, and other forms of documentation, we can chronicle our creative journey, allowing us to revisit and analyze our work critically. This retrospective analysis enables us to identify areas of improvement, discover hidden nuances, and gain a deeper understanding of our artistic choices.

Moreover, documentation allows us to share our work beyond the confines of a live performance. With digital platforms becoming increasingly accessible, we now have the opportunity to reach a wider audience and engage with fellow performers, scholars, and enthusiasts from around the world. By sharing our documented performances, we can inspire others, receive valuable feedback, and foster fruitful collaborations, ultimately broadening our horizons as aspiring performers.

Documentation also plays a crucial role in research and academic contexts. As performance studies students, we are often required to analyze and critique existing performances. Access to well-documented performances provides us with invaluable resources for our studies, allowing us to delve into the intricacies of various artistic approaches, techniques, and theories. By studying documented performances, we can gain insights into different styles, genres, and historical periods, enriching our understanding of the diverse tapestry of performance art.

Lastly, documentation preserves our artistic legacy. As we progress in our performance careers, our documented work serves as a testament to our growth, evolution, and contributions to the field. It allows future generations of performers and scholars to learn from our experiences, building upon the foundations we have laid. By embracing documentation, we ensure that our artistic endeavors leave a lasting impact, creating a legacy that transcends time and space.

In conclusion, documentation is an indispensable tool for students of performance studies. It enhances our understanding, facilitates collaboration, supports academic research, and preserves our artistic legacy. By recognizing the importance of documentation and actively engaging in its practice, we can elevate our performances, contribute to the field, and leave a lasting impact on the world of performance art.

Techniques for Capturing Performances

In the realm of performance studies, capturing and preserving the essence of a live performance is of utmost importance. Whether you are a theater student, a musician, a dancer, or involved in any other form of performance art, finding effective techniques to capture and document your performances can greatly enhance your learning and growth as an artist. This subchapter aims to explore various techniques that students can utilize to capture their performances, allowing them to reflect, analyze, and improve their skills.

One of the most common and accessible methods for capturing performances is through audio recording. By using a simple recording device or even a smartphone, students can easily capture the audio of their performances. This technique allows them to listen back to their performances, identify areas of improvement, and make adjustments accordingly. It is particularly useful for musicians, as they can analyze their technique, timing, and overall musicality.

Another powerful technique for capturing performances is video recording. This method not only captures the audio but also provides a visual representation of the performance. Students can use video recording to observe their body language, facial expressions, and stage presence. This technique is particularly beneficial for theater students, dancers, and any performer who relies heavily on physicality and movement.

In addition to audio and video recording, students can also explore the option of live streaming their performances. With the advancements in technology and the popularity of online platforms, live streaming has become a viable option for capturing performances. By live streaming, students can reach a wider audience, receive instant feedback, and even collaborate with other artists across the globe.

Lastly, for those who prefer a more interactive approach, incorporating audience participation can be an effective technique for capturing performances. Students can encourage their audience to provide feedback, thoughts, and emotions during or after the performance. This technique not only captures the audience's perspective but also fosters a deeper connection between the performer and the observer.

In conclusion, capturing performances is an essential aspect of performance studies. By utilizing techniques such as audio and video recording, live streaming, and audience participation, students can effectively document their performances, allowing for reflection, analysis, and growth. Embracing these techniques will provide students with invaluable tools to master the art of performance, enhance their skills, and become more accomplished artists in their respective fields.

Archiving and Sharing Performance Art

In the realm of performance studies, archiving and sharing performance art is a crucial aspect that often goes overlooked. As students pursuing mastery in the art of performance, it is essential to understand the significance of documenting and preserving our work for future generations. This subchapter aims to shed light on the importance of archiving and sharing performance art, providing students in the field with valuable insights and practical tips.

Archiving performance art serves multiple purposes. Firstly, it allows for the preservation of our artistic endeavors, ensuring that they are not lost or forgotten over time. By capturing and cataloging our performances, we create a legacy that can be referenced and studied by future generations of artists and scholars. Additionally, archiving facilitates the analysis and evaluation of our work, enabling us to reflect on our artistic growth and identify areas for improvement.

When it comes to archiving performance art, there are several methods and mediums to consider. Traditional documentation techniques such as photography and videography can capture the essence of a performance, but it is essential to go beyond mere documentation. Students should explore innovative approaches, such as immersive technologies or interactive digital platforms, to enhance the archival experience. By embracing new technologies, we can create more engaging and immersive archives that effectively convey the essence of our performances.

Sharing performance art is equally important as archiving it. By sharing our work, we extend its reach beyond the confines of a single performance. Through exhibitions, screenings, or online platforms, we enable others to experience and engage with our artistic expressions. Sharing performance art not only fosters dialogue and appreciation but also opens doors for collaborations, networking, and potential career opportunities.

As students, we must actively seek out opportunities to share our work. Local galleries, art festivals, and academic conferences are excellent platforms to showcase our performances. Furthermore, the digital age offers numerous online platforms, social media channels, and video-sharing websites that allow us to reach a global audience. Embracing both physical and virtual avenues of sharing our work maximizes our visibility and impact.

In conclusion, archiving and sharing performance art are vital elements for students in the field of performance studies. By documenting our work, we ensure its preservation and facilitate its analysis. Sharing our performances widens our reach, fostering connections and opening doors for future opportunities. As aspiring artists, let us embrace the responsibility of archiving and sharing our work, contributing to the growth and development of the performance art community.

Chapter 11: Critique and Reflection

The Role of Critique in Performance Art

In the world of performance art, critique plays a vital role in shaping and refining the artistic process. As students of performance studies, it is crucial to understand and embrace the significance of critique in our artistic growth. This subchapter will delve into the various ways critique contributes to the development of performance art, offering invaluable insights for aspiring performers like yourselves.

First and foremost, critique allows us to receive constructive feedback from experienced artists and mentors. By presenting our work to a knowledgeable audience, we gain valuable perspectives on our strengths and weaknesses. This feedback acts as a compass, guiding us towards improvement and providing us with a fresh perspective on our artistic choices. It helps us identify areas that need refinement and encourages us to push our creative boundaries.

Moreover, critique encourages dialogue and collaboration within the performance art community. When we engage in constructive critique sessions, we open ourselves up to diverse viewpoints, expanding our artistic horizons. The exchange of ideas and perspectives fosters a sense of camaraderie among fellow performers, creating a supportive and nurturing environment for growth. Through this process, we not only learn from others but also contribute to the development of the performance art field.

Critique also plays a crucial role in developing our critical thinking skills. As students of performance studies, we must learn to analyze and deconstruct performances, understanding the intentions behind artistic choices. By engaging in thoughtful critique, we sharpen our ability to assess the effectiveness of our own work and that of others. This analytical mindset is essential in creating impactful and thought-provoking performances.

Additionally, critique helps us navigate the complexities of audience reception. Understanding how our work is perceived by different individuals and communities is essential in effectively communicating our artistic ideas. Through critique, we can gauge the audience's response and adapt our performances accordingly, enhancing their overall impact. This valuable feedback allows us to refine our work to resonate more profoundly with our intended audience.

In conclusion, critique is an integral part of the performance art journey. As students of performance studies, we must embrace critique as a tool for growth, pushing ourselves to constantly evolve and refine our craft. By seeking feedback, engaging in dialogue, and sharpening our critical thinking skills, we pave the way for impactful and meaningful performances. Remember, critique is not a judgment, but a stepping stone towards artistic excellence.

Techniques for Giving and Receiving Constructive Feedback

In the world of Performance Studies, constructive feedback is an essential tool for growth and improvement. Whether you are an actor, dancer, musician, or any other type of performer, the ability to give and receive feedback effectively can elevate your skills and help you reach new heights in your craft. This subchapter will explore various techniques for giving and receiving constructive feedback, empowering students in the field of Performance Studies to enhance their abilities and achieve their full potential.

When it comes to giving feedback, it is crucial to maintain a positive and supportive approach. Begin by acknowledging the performer's strengths and highlighting what they did well. This sets a positive tone and creates a safe space for the performer to receive criticism. Be specific in your feedback, focusing on particular moments or techniques that stood out. This specificity allows the performer to understand the areas they should continue to develop or refine. Additionally, offer suggestions for improvement, providing actionable steps that the performer can take to enhance their skills. Remember to always deliver feedback in a respectful and constructive manner, emphasizing the intention to help rather than criticize.

On the receiving end, it is essential to adopt a growth mindset and be open to feedback. Understand that constructive criticism is not a personal attack but an opportunity for growth. Actively listen to the feedback given, taking notes if necessary. Seek clarification if something is unclear, and ask questions to gain a deeper understanding of the feedback. Instead of becoming defensive, embrace the feedback as a chance to learn and improve. Reflect on the feedback and consider how it aligns with your personal goals and aspirations. Use this feedback as a roadmap for your future practice and performances.

In conclusion, mastering the art of giving and receiving constructive feedback is invaluable for any student in the field of Performance Studies. By adopting a positive and supportive approach to giving feedback and maintaining an open mindset when receiving feedback, students can accelerate their growth and development as performers. Embrace feedback as an essential tool for improvement, and use it to refine your skills, overcome challenges, and reach your full potential.

Reflecting on Your Performance Journey

In the world of performance studies, the journey towards mastery is an ongoing process filled with self-discovery, growth, and personal development. As students in this field, it is crucial to take time to reflect on your performance journey, as it can provide valuable insights and enhance your overall learning experience.

Reflection allows you to delve deeper into your performances, both good and bad, and analyze the factors that contributed to your success or challenges. It enables you to understand your strengths, weaknesses, and areas for improvement, thereby aiding your growth as a performer.

One of the primary benefits of reflecting on your performance journey is the opportunity to gain a deeper understanding of yourself as an artist. By critically assessing your performances, you can identify patterns in your work, recognize your unique style, and explore new avenues for artistic expression. This self-awareness is essential in developing your own artistic voice and developing a sense of authenticity in your performances.

Moreover, reflection fosters a sense of accountability. By examining your actions and decisions during performances, you can identify areas where you could have made better choices or taken different approaches. This introspection allows you to become more proactive in your preparation and performance execution, ultimately leading to more successful outcomes.

Reflection also helps you to appreciate the progress you have made on your performance journey. As you look back on previous performances, you may notice how far you have come since the beginning of your studies. Acknowledging your growth can boost your confidence, motivation, and passion for performance, inspiring you to continue pushing boundaries and striving for excellence.

To make the most out of your reflection, consider keeping a performance journal. Document your thoughts, feelings, and observations after each performance, noting both the positive aspects and areas that need improvement. This journal will serve as a valuable resource for future self-reflection and enable you to track your progress over time.

In conclusion, reflecting on your performance journey is an essential aspect of mastering the art of performance. By engaging in self-reflection, you gain self-awareness, develop a sense of accountability, and appreciate your growth as a performer. Embrace this process wholeheartedly and allow it to shape you into the best performer you can be.

Chapter 12: Performance Art in the Digital Age

Exploring the Impact of Technology on Performance Art

Performance art has always been a dynamic and evolving form of artistic expression. Over the years, technology has played an increasingly significant role in shaping and transforming the world of performance art. In this subchapter, we will delve into the fascinating realm of how technology has impacted performance art, and the opportunities it presents to students studying performance studies.

One of the most notable ways technology has influenced performance art is through the integration of multimedia elements. With the advent of digital technology, artists now have access to a wide range of tools and platforms that allow them to incorporate visuals, sound, and interactive elements into their performances. This fusion of different mediums has opened up new avenues for creativity and experimentation, pushing the boundaries of what is possible in performance art.

Furthermore, technology has provided performers with innovative ways to engage with their audience. Live streaming platforms and social media have made it easier for artists to showcase their work to a global audience, breaking down geographical barriers and reaching a wider demographic. This not only increases exposure for aspiring performers but also creates opportunities for collaboration and networking with fellow artists from around the world.

Another significant impact of technology on performance art is the ability to create immersive experiences. Virtual reality (VR) and augmented reality (AR) technologies have revolutionized the way audiences engage with performances. By donning VR headsets or using mobile devices, viewers can now enter a virtual world where they become active participants in the performance. This blurring of the line between reality and art has given rise to a new form of interactive performance art that challenges traditional notions of spectatorship.

However, it is important to acknowledge the potential challenges and ethical considerations that arise with the integration of technology in performance art. Issues such as privacy, consent, and the overreliance on technology can pose significant dilemmas for artists. Therefore, it is crucial for students studying performance studies to critically analyze and navigate these complexities to ensure responsible and impactful use of technology in their work.

In conclusion, technology has undoubtedly had a profound impact on performance art, opening up new possibilities for artistic expression and audience engagement. Students studying performance studies have the opportunity to harness the power of technology to push the boundaries of their craft, creating immersive, multimedia experiences that challenge conventional norms. However, it is essential to approach this integration with a critical and ethical lens, ensuring that technology enhances rather than detracts from the essence of performance art.

Utilizing Digital Platforms for Performance Art

In today's digital age, the world of performance art is evolving rapidly. With the advent of various digital platforms, performers now have the opportunity to reach wider audiences and explore new creative possibilities. This subchapter aims to explore how students in the field of performance studies can harness the power of digital platforms to enhance their artistic practice and engage with their audience in innovative ways.

One of the most exciting aspects of utilizing digital platforms for performance art is the ability to transcend geographical boundaries. Through live streaming or prerecorded performances, students can showcase their work to audiences around the world, breaking down the limitations of physical space. This not only expands the reach of their art but also allows for cultural exchange and collaboration with artists from different backgrounds.

Additionally, digital platforms offer endless possibilities for experimentation and interactivity. Students can explore immersive technologies such as virtual reality or augmented reality to create unique and engaging performance experiences. They can also incorporate elements of interactivity through online platforms, enabling audience participation and feedback in real-time. This dynamic interaction between performer and viewer opens up new avenues for exploration and pushes the boundaries of traditional performance art.

Furthermore, digital platforms provide students with opportunities for documentation and preservation of their work. By recording performances and sharing them online, students can create a digital portfolio that showcases their artistic growth and serves as a valuable resource for future endeavors. This not only helps in building a professional profile but also contributes to the preservation of performance art history.

However, it is important for students to approach digital platforms with a critical eye. While these platforms offer numerous benefits, they also come with their own set of challenges. Students must be mindful of issues such as copyright infringement, privacy concerns, and the potential for digital fatigue. It is crucial to strike a balance between utilizing digital tools and maintaining the authenticity and integrity of the performance art form.

In conclusion, the utilization of digital platforms has revolutionized the field of performance art, offering students in performance studies unprecedented opportunities for growth and exploration. By embracing these platforms, students can engage with a global audience, experiment with new technologies, and document their artistic journey. However, they must also navigate the challenges that come with digital platforms and ensure that the essence of performance art is preserved. With a clear understanding of the potential and pitfalls of digital platforms, students can truly master the art of performance in the modern age.

Navigating Ethical Considerations in the Digital Space

In today's digital age, the boundaries between our personal and professional lives are becoming increasingly blurred. As students in the field of Performance Studies, it is essential that we understand and navigate the ethical considerations that arise in the digital space. This subchapter will explore the various challenges and opportunities presented by the digital world and provide guidance on how to maintain ethical standards while leveraging its potential.

One of the primary ethical concerns in the digital space is the issue of privacy. With the proliferation of social media platforms and online communication channels, it is crucial for students to understand the importance of safeguarding personal information and respecting the privacy of others. We will delve into topics such as managing privacy settings, being mindful of the content we share online, and seeking explicit consent when using someone else's work or image.

Another significant consideration is the responsible use of digital resources. As students in Performance Studies, we often rely on online platforms for research, collaboration, and showcasing our work. However, it is imperative to understand copyright laws, intellectual property rights, and proper citation practices to avoid plagiarism and respect the work of others. We will explore strategies for conducting ethical research, citing sources accurately, and giving credit where it is due.

Furthermore, the digital space poses unique challenges in terms of cyberbullying, harassment, and online etiquette. We will discuss strategies for fostering a positive and inclusive online environment, such as promoting respectful dialogue, combating online negativity, and addressing cyberbullying incidents. It is essential for students to understand the impact of their online presence and actively contribute to a safe and supportive digital community.

Lastly, we will explore the ethical considerations related to digital performances and representations. With the rise of livestreaming, virtual reality, and digital archives, the boundaries of performance are expanding. Students must grapple with questions of authenticity, representation, and cultural appropriation. We will examine case studies and engage in critical discussions to develop a nuanced understanding of these complex issues.

In conclusion, the digital space offers numerous opportunities and challenges for students in Performance Studies. By navigating ethical considerations in the digital space, we can harness its potential while upholding our professional and personal integrity. This subchapter equips students with the knowledge and tools needed to make informed decisions, foster online ethics, and contribute positively to the digital landscape.

Chapter 13: Performance Art in Different Contexts

Performance Art in Educational Settings

Performance art is a dynamic and captivating form of artistic expression that has the power to engage and challenge both the performer and the audience. In recent years, it has gained significant recognition and popularity in educational settings, particularly within the field of performance studies. This subchapter aims to explore the unique role of performance art in educational settings and how it can enhance the learning experience for students in this niche.

One of the key advantages of incorporating performance art into educational settings is its ability to provide a hands-on and experiential learning experience. Unlike traditional lecture-based methods, performance art allows students to actively participate and engage with the material being taught. Through performance, students can embody and express complex ideas, emotions, and concepts, making the learning process more immersive and memorable.

Furthermore, performance art encourages creativity and self-expression, allowing students to develop their artistic abilities and explore their unique artistic voice. It provides a platform for students to experiment with different performance techniques, styles, and mediums, fostering a sense of artistic freedom and exploration. This not only benefits students in performance studies but also those pursuing other disciplines, as performance art can be a valuable tool for self-expression and personal growth.

In addition to its educational benefits, performance art in educational settings also serves as a means of fostering community and collaboration. Students engage in group performances, workshops, and collaborative projects, building strong bonds and relationships with their peers. This collaborative aspect of performance art promotes teamwork, communication, and empathy, essential skills that are transferable to various aspects of life.

Moreover, performance art in educational settings offers students the opportunity to engage with diverse perspectives and challenge societal norms and conventions. Through performances that address social, cultural, and political issues, students can develop a critical understanding of the world around them and actively participate in important conversations.

In conclusion, performance art in educational settings holds immense potential for students in the field of performance studies. By providing an experiential and hands-on learning experience, encouraging creativity and self-expression, fostering collaboration, and promoting critical thinking, performance art enhances the educational journey of students. So, embrace the power of performance art and unleash your artistic potential!

Performance Art in Public Spaces

Performance art is a unique form of artistic expression that has gained significant popularity in recent years. It involves the creation and presentation of live performances by artists, often in unconventional spaces such as public parks, city streets, or abandoned buildings. This subchapter explores the concept of performance art in public spaces, delving into its significance, challenges, and impact on both the artists and the audience.

Performing in public spaces provides artists with an opportunity to engage directly with the community and break away from the traditional confines of a theater or gallery. This allows for a more intimate and immersive experience, as the performance becomes a part of people's daily lives. By taking their art to the streets, performance artists challenge societal norms and provoke thought and discussion among the audience.

One of the primary advantages of performing in public spaces is the accessibility it offers. Unlike traditional art forms, which often require a ticket or specific venue, performance art in public spaces is free and available to everyone. This inclusivity enables a diverse range of audiences to experience and engage with the art, fostering a sense of community and shared experience.

However, performing in public spaces also presents unique challenges for artists. They must navigate logistical issues such as obtaining permits, managing technical requirements, and addressing potential disruptions from the public. Additionally, the lack of a controlled environment means that unexpected factors, such as weather conditions or unexpected noise, can impact the performance. Nonetheless, these challenges can also foster creativity and adaptability, pushing artists to think outside the box and find innovative ways to overcome obstacles.

Performance art in public spaces has the power to transform the perception of the urban environment and challenge traditional notions of art. By bringing art into the public realm, it blurs the boundaries between the artist and the audience, creating a shared experience that is both personal and collective. It encourages individuals to question their surroundings, their role in society, and their relationship with art.

For students studying performance studies, exploring performance art in public spaces opens up a world of possibilities. It allows them to understand the social, cultural, and political implications of their work. By engaging with the public, students can gain valuable insights into the impact of their performances and learn how to navigate the challenges and opportunities that arise in non-traditional spaces.

In conclusion, performance art in public spaces is a dynamic and exciting form of artistic expression. It offers unique opportunities for artists to engage with the community, challenge norms, and create a shared experience. For students studying performance studies, delving into this aspect of performance art can broaden their horizons and equip them with the skills needed to excel in this evolving field.

Performance Art in Cultural and Community Events

In the realm of performance studies, one cannot overlook the significant role performance art plays in cultural and community events. Performance art is a unique form of artistic expression that combines various elements such as music, dance, theater, and visual arts to create a thought-provoking and immersive experience for both the performers and the audience. In this subchapter, we will explore the fascinating world of performance art in cultural and community events, delving into its impact, significance, and the opportunities it presents for students in the field of performance studies.

Cultural and community events are the perfect platform for performance art to thrive. These events bring people from diverse backgrounds together, fostering a sense of unity, understanding, and appreciation for different cultures and traditions. Performance art, with its ability to transcend language barriers and communicate on an emotional level, becomes a powerful tool in promoting cultural exchange and dialogue. Students studying performance art have a unique opportunity to contribute to these events, showcasing their talent and creativity while also bridging gaps between communities.

Participating in cultural and community events not only provides students with valuable performance experience but also allows them to engage with the audience and receive feedback. This interaction helps students refine their craft, understand the impact of their art on others, and develop a deeper connection with their audience. Moreover, being part of such events exposes students to a wide range of artistic styles and influences, expanding their horizons and encouraging experimentation in their own work.

Performance art in cultural and community events also serves as a catalyst for social change and activism. By addressing important social issues through their art, students can raise awareness, provoke discussions, and inspire action. Performance art has the power to challenge societal norms, question authority, and give a voice to marginalized communities. Through their performances, students can become agents of change, advocating for inclusivity, equality, and justice.

In conclusion, performance art in cultural and community events is a vital aspect of the field of performance studies. The ability of performance art to transcend boundaries and foster understanding makes it an essential tool in promoting cultural exchange and unity. Moreover, students studying performance art have the opportunity to showcase their talent, engage with the audience, and contribute to social change. By participating in cultural and community events, students can enhance their skills, broaden their artistic influences, and make a meaningful impact on society. Embracing performance art in these events is an essential step in mastering the art of performance.

Chapter 14: Taking Your Performance Art to the Next Level

Pursuing Further Education and Training

In the field of Performance Studies, the journey of mastering the art of performance is an ongoing one. As students, we embark on this path with a burning passion for the arts and a desire to push ourselves beyond our limits. However, to truly excel in this field, it is crucial to understand the importance of pursuing further education and training.

Further education serves as a stepping stone towards honing our skills and expanding our artistic horizons. It provides us with a deeper understanding of the theories and concepts that underpin performance, enabling us to develop a critical eye and a comprehensive knowledge base. By immersing ourselves in academic courses, such as theatre history, acting techniques, or dance composition, we gain a broader perspective that enhances our ability to interpret and convey emotions on stage.

Additionally, further education also allows us to explore specialized areas within performance studies. Whether it is stage management, lighting design, or costume construction, delving into these specific disciplines helps us cultivate a well-rounded skill set. When we have expertise in multiple areas, we become more versatile performers, capable of adapting to diverse roles and collaborating effectively with other professionals in the industry.

Training, on the other hand, is the practical counterpart to education. While education equips us with knowledge, training provides us with the tools to apply that knowledge effectively. It is through rigorous training that we refine our technique, develop physical stamina, and build the discipline necessary for a successful career in performance. Whether it is through daily practice, workshops, or intensive programs, consistent training helps us stay in peak condition, both physically and mentally.

Moreover, pursuing further education and training also presents us with invaluable networking opportunities. Within academic institutions and training programs, we meet like-minded individuals who share our passion for the performing arts. These connections can lead to collaborations, mentorship, and future career opportunities. By surrounding ourselves with a supportive and diverse community, we gain inspiration, learn from others' experiences, and continue to grow as artists.

In conclusion, pursuing further education and training is a vital aspect of mastering the art of performance. It broadens our knowledge base, allows us to specialize in specific disciplines, hones our skills, and opens doors to valuable connections. As students in the field of Performance Studies, we must recognize the importance of continuous learning and training to reach our full potential and achieve excellence in our chosen craft.

Exploring Career Opportunities in Performance Art

In today's ever-evolving world, the field of performance art offers an array of exciting and diverse career opportunities for students specializing in Performance Studies. Whether you have a passion for acting, dancing, singing, or any other form of artistic expression, this subchapter will guide you through the various paths you can pursue within the realm of performance art.

1. Acting: For those with a flair for the dramatic, a career in acting can be immensely fulfilling. Whether on stage or screen, actors bring stories and characters to life, captivating audiences with their talent and dedication. Opportunities in theater, film, television, and even voice acting are abundant, providing a range of avenues to explore your craft.

2. Dance: If your passion lies in movement and rhythm, pursuing a career in dance can open doors to a world of creativity. From classical ballet to contemporary styles, there are numerous opportunities to perform with renowned dance companies, join theater productions, or even become a choreographer, teaching others the art of movement.

3. Musical Theater: Combining the elements of acting, singing, and dancing, musical theater offers an exciting career path for those who possess multiple talents. Auditioning for Broadway shows, touring companies, or even working in regional theaters can provide a platform to showcase your skills and immerse yourself in the magical world of musical storytelling.

4. Performance Art Installations: For those interested in pushing the boundaries of traditional performance, the world of performance art

installations offers a unique avenue for expression. Creating immersive experiences through visual, auditory, and interactive elements, performance art installations challenge perceptions and provoke thought.

5. Performance Art Education: If sharing your passion and knowledge with others is a calling, a career in performance art education might be the right path for you. Teaching in schools, universities, or even starting your own workshops and classes allows you to inspire and mentor future generations of performers.

6. Arts Administration: Behind every successful performance, there is a team of professionals working tirelessly to make it happen. Pursuing a career in arts administration allows you to contribute to the industry by managing theaters, coordinating events, marketing performances, or even working in talent agencies.

Remember, the field of performance art is vast and constantly evolving. It is essential to stay open to new opportunities, network with industry professionals, and continuously develop your skills. Exploring career opportunities in performance art can be an exhilarating journey, full of challenges and rewards. However, with dedication, passion, and a strong foundation in Performance Studies, you can master the art of performance and create a fulfilling career in this captivating field.

Continuing to Grow and Evolve as a Performer

As students of performance studies, we are always striving to improve and reach new heights in our craft. The journey to becoming a master performer is a lifelong process, filled with challenges and opportunities for growth. In this subchapter, we will explore the importance of continuing to grow and evolve as a performer and how it can positively impact our artistic journey.

One of the key aspects of growth as a performer is the willingness to step out of our comfort zones. It is easy to stick to what we know and feel comfortable with, but true growth occurs when we push ourselves beyond our limits. Trying new genres, experimenting with different techniques, and exploring diverse styles of performance can open up new avenues of creativity and expand our artistic horizons.

Additionally, seeking feedback and constructive criticism is crucial for growth. As students, we have the unique advantage of having mentors and instructors who can provide valuable insights and guidance. By actively seeking feedback and implementing the suggestions provided, we can refine our skills and address any weaknesses or areas for improvement.

Furthermore, engaging in continuous learning is vital for the growth of a performer. This includes attending workshops, masterclasses, and seminars, as well as reading books and articles on performance theory and practice. By staying updated with the latest trends and developments in the field, we can adapt our performances to resonate with contemporary audiences and remain relevant in a rapidly evolving industry.

Collaboration is also a powerful tool for growth. Working with other performers, directors, and designers can expose us to different perspectives and techniques. Through collaboration, we can learn from one another, build lasting relationships, and develop a deeper understanding of the collaborative nature of performance.

Lastly, it is essential to remember that growth as a performer is not solely dependent on external factors. It also requires self-reflection and introspection. Taking the time to analyze our performances, identify our strengths and weaknesses, and set realistic goals can greatly contribute to our growth as performers.

In conclusion, the journey to mastering the art of performance is a continuous process of growth and evolution. By stepping out of our comfort zones, seeking feedback, pursuing continuous learning, collaborating with others, and engaging in self-reflection, we can enhance our skills and become the best performers we can be. Embrace the challenges and opportunities for growth, and watch yourself transform into a truly remarkable performer.

Chapter 15: Conclusion

Recapitulating the Journey of Mastering Performance Art

As students of performance studies, we embark on a journey to master the art of performance, aiming to express ourselves creatively and captivate audiences with our unique talents. Along this path, we encounter various challenges, triumphs, and moments of self-discovery. In this subchapter, we recapitulate the transformative journey we have undertaken, highlighting the key lessons and experiences that have shaped us as performers.

The journey of mastering performance art begins with self-reflection and introspection. We delve into understanding our strengths, weaknesses, and passions, as these will form the foundation of our artistic expression. Through rigorous training and practice, we refine our technical skills and develop a strong command over our chosen art form, be it dance, theater, music, or any other medium.

However, mastering performance art extends beyond technical proficiency. It requires us to explore our emotional intelligence, connecting deeply with our characters or the essence of our chosen performance style. We learn to embody different personalities, channeling their emotions and experiences, allowing the audience to experience a range of human emotions through our performances.

Throughout this journey, we encounter setbacks and obstacles that test our resilience and determination. We learn that failure is not the end, but rather an opportunity for growth. Each stumble becomes a stepping stone towards improvement, as we cultivate a mindset of continuous learning and improvement.

Collaboration is another crucial aspect of mastering performance art. We discover the power of teamwork, realizing that great performances are often the result of collective effort. Working alongside fellow students, we learn to communicate effectively, share ideas, and adapt to different working styles. Through collaboration, we gain a broader perspective and open ourselves to new possibilities, collectively pushing the boundaries of our creativity.

As we progress, we also learn the importance of self-care and maintaining a healthy work-life balance. The rigorous demands of performance art can take a toll on our physical and mental well-being. We understand the significance of nurturing ourselves, physically and emotionally, to sustain our passion and drive for the art.

Ultimately, the journey of mastering performance art is a personal and transformative one. It is a process of self-discovery, growth, and self-expression. Each step we take brings us closer to becoming the best versions of ourselves as performers. As students of performance studies, we are fortunate to be on this path, continuously honing our skills and enriching our understanding of this exquisite art form. Let this recapitulation remind us of the incredible journey we have undertaken and inspire us to continue pushing the boundaries of our artistic capabilities.

Encouragement and Inspiration for Future Performers

As students pursuing a degree in performance studies, we are embarking on a journey that requires immense dedication, perseverance, and passion. The road to becoming a successful performer is not an easy one, but with the right mindset and a few words of encouragement, we can overcome the challenges and reach our full potential.

First and foremost, it is crucial to believe in yourself and your abilities. Confidence is key when it comes to performing on stage or in any artistic endeavor. Remember that you have been chosen for this path because you possess a unique gift and talent. Embrace it, nurture it, and let it shine. Trust in your training and the countless hours you have dedicated to honing your craft.

However, it is important to acknowledge that setbacks and failures are a part of the journey. Every performer has faced moments of doubt and disappointment. These experiences should not discourage you but serve as stepping stones for growth and improvement. Learn from your mistakes, seek feedback from mentors and peers, and use these lessons to become a stronger performer.

Additionally, it is essential to find inspiration from the world around you. Seek out performances, whether it be in theater, dance, or music, that move and captivate you. Attend concerts, watch films, and read books that ignite your imagination and expand your understanding of the arts. Surround yourself with like-minded individuals who share your passion, as they can provide support, motivation, and valuable insights.

Remember that success in performance studies is not solely measured by achieving fame or recognition. It is about finding joy and fulfillment in the act of performing and connecting with an audience. Embrace the process, relish in each moment on stage, and allow yourself to be vulnerable. It is through vulnerability that true artistry is born.

Lastly, never lose sight of why you chose this path. As performers, we have the incredible power to touch the hearts and souls of those who witness our craft. Whether it is through laughter, tears, or contemplation, our performances can inspire, provoke thought, and spark change. Always remember the impact you can have on others and the world around you.

In conclusion, dear students of performance studies, you have chosen a challenging yet rewarding path. Believe in yourself, learn from setbacks, find inspiration in the world, and never lose sight of the profound impact you can make. Embrace the journey, for it is through dedication and passion that you will truly master the art of performance.

Final Thoughts on the Art of Performance

As we come to the end of this journey through the world of performance, it is important to reflect on the lessons we have learned and the wisdom we have gained. The art of performance is a multifaceted discipline that requires dedication, skill, and a deep understanding of oneself as both an artist and a human being.

Throughout this book, we have explored various aspects of performance studies, from the foundational techniques to the nuances of interpretation. We have delved into the importance of breath control, physicality, and vocal projection, and we have examined the power of storytelling and the impact it can have on an audience. But beyond the technical aspects, we have also discussed the emotional journey of a performer, the vulnerability required to fully embody a character, and the connection that can be forged between performer and audience.

Now, as you embark on your own journeys in performance, I urge you to remember a few key points. Firstly, never lose sight of the joy and passion that brought you to this art form in the first place. Performance is a privilege and a gift, and it is important to approach it with a sense of wonder and gratitude.

Secondly, embrace failure as an opportunity for growth. Performance is inherently risky, and not every moment will be perfect. But it is through these moments of imperfection that we learn the most about ourselves and our craft. Embrace the mistakes, learn from them, and allow them to propel you forward.

Lastly, remember that your voice matters. As a performer, you have a unique perspective to share with the world. Whether it is through the characters you portray or the stories you tell, you have the power to inspire, educate, and entertain. Do not shy away from using your voice to make a difference.

In conclusion, mastering the art of performance is a lifelong journey. It is a constant exploration of self, of technique, and of the human condition. As students of performance studies, you have chosen a path that requires discipline, dedication, and a deep love for the craft. Embrace the challenges, celebrate the victories, and always remember that the art of performance has the power to change lives – both yours and those of your audience. So go forth, my fellow students, and let your performances be a testament to the beauty and power of the human spirit.

www.ingramcontent.com/pod-product-compliance
Lightning Source LLC
LaVergne TN
LVHW020924200726
843506LV00011B/1800